Samuel Abbot Smith

West Cambridge on the Nineteenth of April, 1775

An address delivered in behalf of the Ladies' Soldiers' Aid Society of West

Cambridge

Samuel Abbot Smith

West Cambridge on the Nineteenth of April, 1775
An address delivered in behalf of the Ladies' Soldiers' Aid Society of West Cambridge

ISBN/EAN: 9783337307998

Printed in Europe, USA, Canada, Australia, Japan

Cover: Foto ©ninafisch / pixelio.de

More available books at **www.hansebooks.com**

West Cambridge on the Nineteenth of April, 1775

AN ADDRESS

DELIVERED IN BEHALF OF THE

LADIES' SOLDIERS' AID SOCIETY

OF WEST CAMBRIDGE

BY SAMUEL ABBOT SMITH

BOSTON

ALFRED MUDGE & SON, PRINTERS, 34 SCHOOL STREET

1864

ADDRESS.

In these stirring and momentous times, the platform becomes almost as serious as the pulpit. A man should be ashamed to stand before his countrymen, and certainly before his countrywomen, to deliver a mere literary disquisition. Our hearts cannot but throb in unison with the beatings of the national heart; our words in some way must deal with the great interests of the time, or they will fall on listless ears. We cannot forget, even in this quiet hour together, that our nation is in her great trial, and that a million of our brothers are offering themselves a sacrifice, if need be, for the safety of our country and of us all.

It seems to me that the present is an appropriate time for reviewing together the events of that world-famed day, when the tide of war surged through these quiet streets of ours; for recalling the sacri-

fices and heroism of the " times which tried men's
souls " as to-day tries them.   I would refresh the
memory of the old with the repetition of those tales
of patriotic devotion which they heard from parents'
lips; I would tell the young that these hills and
these streets are holy ground, consecrate with earth's
most precious thing, — the blood of heroes, — that
perchance the sacred flame may be kindled in their
hearts, and they may be heroes too.   I would repeat
the story of that memorable day, the Nineteenth of
April, 1775, endeavoring especially to illustrate the
part our own town took in it, gathering up the fast-
fading traditions from those lips soon to be sealed
forever.   But one * remains here now of all those
who saw the sun of that bright April morning.

West Cambridge has not yet had justice done her
for the part she took in those scenes.   Histories and
orations have had little to say about her.   It has
been the " Battle of Lexington and Concord; " it
should be the " Battle of Concord, Lexington, and
West Cambridge."   Within our town the battle
raged fiercest; more than a third of the patriots

* Mrs. Lydia Peirce.

who died that day, fell within our limits. We have more precious dust garnered under yonder stone, than any other town has treasured beneath its monument.

Let us, then, to-night, standing here on this historic ground, this very spot where British and American bullets once crossed each other with deadly aim, close to which the first capture of the Revolution was made, let us remember our Fathers.

The memorable year 1775 opened gloomily. The public mind was in a state of extreme irritation throughout the colonies, and only a spark was required to set all in a flame. There was no disposition to redress grievances on the part of the crown; the arbitrary and oppressive acts of the royal governor called forth constantly more strenuous, but so far only passive, resistance on the part of the people, and yet both alike were shrinking from the last resort.

I find in the note-book of Samuel Cooke, first pastor of this parish, which he kept mostly in Latin, a few remarks which perhaps may be interesting as showing the general state of things at this time.

1 *

Under date of Jan. 31, 1775, he thus sums up the account of the month:

"Ends with moderate weather, as it has been through ye month. Some rain, no snow. A turn of good sledding in the great roads. A vast quantity of snow which fell last month, very much drifted. Wood dear, provisions plenty and cheap. Rie, 28 to 30s; Indian, 27s; Beef, 2s 2d; Pork, 2s.* Speech delivered in P——t by George III. The Lord reigneth! Tories employing their envenomed pens to secure and acquire places and pensions, to terrific and divide the people. O Lord, turn their counsels into foolishness!"

In February the Legislature of Massachusetts, which, after its dissolution by the governor, had met independently of his authority as the Provincial Congress, appointed eleven men as a Committee of Safety, Joseph Warren at its head. They were to

---

* I have no means of ascertaining the exact value of the shilling at this time; probably it did not vary much from the year 1740, when Mr. Cooke writes that boarding with Dea. Joseph Adams, he paid 10s per week, at the rate of 26s to the ounce of silver.

take charge of the warlike stores of the province, to enroll the militia, and muster into active service as many as they might think advisable. Officers were also appointed to take command of this provincial army when assembled. Throughout Massachusetts, indeed through the thirteen colonies, the people were assiduously practising the use of arms, and engaging in military exercises. The clergy were not behind their people in zeal and patriotism.

I hold in my hand a sermon preached in the old church yonder,* by the pastor, Rev. Samuel Cooke, to the minute company of West Cambridge, about a month before the battle.

Text, Nehemiah 4: 13, 14, 15. " * * * Be not ye afraid of them: remember the Lord, which is great and terrible, and fight for your brethren, your sons, and your daughters, your wives, and your houses. And it came to pass when our enemies heard that it was known unto us, and God had

---

* This building still stands on Pleasant street, and is now the residence of Mr. Charles Gage. It gave place to a larger edifice early in this century, being then removed and changed into a dwelling house.

brought their counsel to nought, that we returned all of us to the wall, every one unto his work."

"The appearance of arms in this religious assembly reminds me of that expression of the Roman orator, 'Quanquam præsidiis salutaribus et necessariis septi sumus,' etc., which we may thus translate, 'Though we are surrounded with safe and necessary guards, yet the means of safety awakens our fears.'"

"These instruments of death, taken up only for our necessary defence under alarming threats, we heartily wish and pray may not be prepared for the day of battle, but a happy means to prevent the conflicting warriors, confused noise, and garments rolled in blood. Similar preparations for defence to those now making through this land, happily operated to the complete deliverance of the Jews, without the hazard of an engagement. And this instance is recorded for our encouragement, while we are satisfied our cause is just. We feel ourselves sensibly interested in the distresses of these Jews, as, in some respects, they bear a near resemblance to our own."

He goes on to describe the situation of the Jews, settled in a country distant from the seat of sovereign power, whither they had removed by royal permission with ample charter privileges. The king, misled by their enemies, had issued decrees, oppressive and subversive of their chartered rights.

These unjust decrees being disobeyed, a force was sent out to compel obedience. The wise and spirited precautions taken by the patriot ruler of the Jews are worthy of observation. 1st. They asked the divine protection. They did not, however, presume on this protection without the use of the proper means. 2d. They set a watch. 3d. They armed themselves for a vigorous defence in case of attack. "It does not appear," he says, "that they were so unhappy as to have any *traitorous sons* within their walls, but that some were terrified with the sound of arms and the alarms of war."

After applying still more at length the example of the Jewish people and their ruler, and remarking on the success of these measures, he goes on to say:

"And now, brethren, the case we have been considering is recorded for our instruction. It is with the deepest regret that we in any degree apply these to ourselves in the present gloomy day. The adversaries of Judah were foreigners, they were Pagans. These like horrible attempts constrain us to say, that Britons are our adversaries! That Englishmen thirst for our blood! That our most gracious sovereign George III. declares us rebels!* Our adversaries, we may conclude, have long, by repeated insults, endeavored to provoke us to some act that might be represented as rebellious, but disappointment appears only to have enhanced their rage; and the vengeance long since imprecated by one born among us is now pointed at our breasts.

The steps directed by the grand Continental Congress we have attended to, trusting, under God, for safety in their judicious and united counsels. But their loyal and spirited address to the throne appears to have proved ineffectual. It remains for us to pursue the measures with vigor, they have advised to, as our last resort.

There at present appears no other choice left us,

* The words "God forbid!" are written after the word rebels, but they are partially erased in the manuscript.

but either tamely to sit down and surrender our
lives and properties, our wives and children, our
religion and consciences, to the arbitrary will of
others, or, trusting in God, to stand up in our own
defence, and of the British Constitution."

Noble words were these in a noble cause! We
need not wonder that the men of that day were
brave and patriotic, when they received such counsels from their religious teachers.

The aggressions of the British continued, and
things every day more clearly indicated that an
appeal to arms was near at hand. Boston Neck
was fortified. An unsuccessful attempt was made
by British troops to seize the cannon deposited at
Salem. Officers were sent out in disguise to make
sketches of the roads, and ascertain the state of the
towns. Eleven hundred men marched out of Boston
and threw down the stone walls in the neighborhood,
thus preparing a field for any future emergency.

The news from Europe also wore a hostile aspect.
The ministry had determined to compel the colonies
to obedience. The Americans were looked upon as
cowards, and it was said that five regiments of regulars could easily march across the continent.

Nor were preparations lacking upon our side.
The men capable of bearing arms organized themselves into companies, and there were enough veter-
ans, who had seen military service in the French
war, to act as their leaders.* The Committee of
Safety took the general charge of these preparations, and had collected a large amount of military
stores at Concord.

On Saturday, the fifteenth of April, the Provincial
Congress which had been holding its meeting at
Concord adjourned to the tenth of May. General
Gage, having just received a small reinforcement,
had now under his command in Boston between
three and four thousand veteran troops. He thought
that the time had come at last for action, and with
one decisive blow he hoped to crush the spirit of
rebellion. On that very Saturday afternoon the
grenadiers and light infantry were relieved from
garrison duty in Boston, and concentrated on the
Common, under pretence of learning a new military

* Rev. Mr. Cooke preached a sermon Nov. 12, 1758, upon the
occasion of the return of Capt. Adams and company, with the
loss of only a single man.

exercise. At midnight the boats of the transports were collected and moored under the protection of the ships of war. These movements seemed suspicious, and Warren sent word at once to Hancock and Adams, who were then at Lexington; through this timely intelligence the cannon were secreted and some of the stores removed from Concord on the seventeenth. On Tuesday Gen. Gage sent out ten sergeants to Cambridge, who, after dining there, at night scattered themselves along the various roads leading out of Boston, in order to cut off all communication with the country. At ten o'clock the following evening the grenadiers and light infantry, eight hundred in number, embarked on the boats of the transports at the foot of the Common under command of Lieut. Col. Smith. Every movement was watched, and at once Warren sent a messenger through Roxbury to Lexington, and Paul Revere was rowed across almost under the guns of the Somerset man-of-war to Charlestown, only a few minutes before the sentinels received orders to allow no American to pass the lines. He narrowly escaped being captured in Charlestown by some of

2

the British officers on the road, and passed on to Medford, awaking there the captain of the minute men. thence he pursued his way through West Cambridge to Lexington, giving the alarm at almost every house on the road.

The troops crossed the bay in the boats of the squadron, and landed at East Cambridge, near where the court-house now stands. Here they received a day's rations, and, taking the path across the marshes, where in some places they were obliged to wade through the water, they entered the old West Cambridge and Charlestown road (or Milkrow, as we call it), at the foot of Prospect Hill.

It was nearly two o'clock in the morning when they entered the limits of Menotomy. as this northwest precinct of Cambridge was then called. They marched under those two old elms which still form the beautiful eastern gate-way of our town. Long may they stand, and may never an enemy's foot again tread beneath them! They marched on stealthily, and, as they thought, in secret; but watchful eyes were upon them. The old man, Samuel Whittemore, lived with his son and his grand-

children, in the house under the shade of the old
elms, just this side of the brook which divides us
now from Cambridge. He was awakened by the
stir in the street, and looking out saw the bayonets
glistening in the moonlight. As they made their
hasty preparations in the morning, the lad Amos,
afterwards distinguished as the inventor of the
card-machine, brought out two or three old guns,
which, perhaps, had done good service in the
French war, but had long before been thrown
aside as useless. He had repaired the broken
locks, and made them ready for deadly service,
and now the boy of sixteen wished to go and bear
his part with the rest. But Amos was obliged to
remain to take care of his mother and the children,
while the old grandfather and the son and the elder
boys engaged in the fight.*

The Committee of Safety, on the day before (the
eighteenth) had held their session at the Black
Horse tavern in West Cambridge, kept by Weth-
erby, which stood near the site of the old alms-
house. The other members of that body had

* Mrs. Henry Whittemore.

returned to their homes at the close of the meeting; but three of them, Vice-President Gerry and Cols. Lee and Orne, spent the night here, and arose from their beds to view the unwonted sight. They watched the soldiers passing by, till, as the centre was opposite, an officer and a file of men were detached to search the house. This movement first gave them the hint of danger, and they hurried down stairs. Gerry in his perturbation being on the point of opening the front door in their faces, when the landlord cried out to him, "For God's sake don't open that door!" and led them to the back part of the house, whence they escaped into the corn-field, before the officer had posted his guards about the doors. There was nothing to conceal them from view in the broad field but the corn-stubble which had been left the previous fall a foot or two high, and that was little protection in the bright moonlight. Gerry stumbled and fell, and called out to his friend, "Stop, Orne; stop for me till I can get up; I have hurt myself!" This suggested the idea, and they all threw themselves flat on the ground, and, concealed by the stubble,

remained there. half-clothed as they had left their
beds. till the troops passed on. Col. Lee never
recovered from the effects of that midnight expos-
ure; he died in less than a month from that night.
The house was searched in vain, though they found
the beds which the objects of their pursuit had just
left, and a gold watch belonging to one of them
under the pillow, which they did not carry away.*

The man who lived in the house recently torn
down by Mr. Allen, was awakened by the rattle of
the pewter plates on his dresser. jarred, as they
were, by the measured tramp of soldiers, and hasten-
ing to the window, saw his yard full of red-coats,
who had been getting water from his well. He stole
down stairs to secure his gun. which he hid in the
chimney; and in the morning, after clearing the
house of valuables, so far as he could, he sent his
family to Geo. Prentiss' on the hill, and himself
joined the minute men.

Solomon Bowman, the lieutenant of the minute

* Miss Orne, who received this account from the lips of her
grandmother, who was niece of Elbridge Gerry, and daughter-
in-law of Col. Orne.

2*

company, lived in the house now occupied by Mrs. Henry Whittemore. He was on the alert, and came to the door to see what was stirring. A soldier, leaving the ranks, asked him for a drink of water; he refused, saying, " What are you out, at this time of night, for ? " As soon as they passed, he at once began to warn the company, and at day-break they were formed on the common ready for active service.*

The house opposite, lately destroyed by fire, had its chimneys painted white, the sign, in those days, that its occupant was a tory. The British met a more gracious reception there, than across the street, and were directed on their way.†

They paused a moment at the centre of the town, and the British commander, finding that the country was thoroughly aroused, despatched his light infantry in advance for the purpose of securing the Concord bridges, and sent back to Gen. Gage for reinforcements, — a piece of prudence which alone saved his whole force from destruction. In silence they resumed their march. Mr. Cutter, who lived in the

* Mrs. Hill, daughter of Lieut. Bowman.
† Mrs. Henry Whittemore and Mrs. Dr. Wellington.

house now the westerly end of the upper tavern, looked around for his gun, as he saw the soldiers open his barn doors and look at his favorite horse, but he had lent it the day before, much to his wife's joy.

Though it was so long after midnight, some young men were busily engaged playing cards in a shop which used to stand in front of where James Schouler now lives, and they did not leave their game till they were startled by the near approach of the British troops.*

They saw the glimmer of a light through the shutter of the house, still standing at the upper corner of the road which leads to Winchester; a soldier was sent to inquire the meaning of a light at this unusual hour. The wife replied that her "old man was sick, and she was making some herb tea." The soldier was satisfied with the answer, and rejoined his comrades.

But the old shoemaker and his wife had just been melting their pewter plates into bullets, and when startled by the loud knock at the door, the old man

* A. R. Proctor, who heard it from William Hill.

had thrown himself upon the bed, and his wife had
upset the skillet of molten lead into the turf ashes,
before she unlocked the door.   Before the next
night, no doubt, some of those so proudly marching
by, tasted of that herb tea to their sorrow.*

Before day-break the next morning all in West
Cambridge knew what had happened, and they
bravely prepared for the emergency.   Those on the
line of the great road, secured their most valuable
possessions, in many cases throwing their pewter
plates and their silver into the wells.   The women
and children were removed to places of safety.
Some went down to Mystic river, others to the
borders of Winchester, and many gathered at Geo.
Prentiss' on the hill.   His daughter,† yet surviving
at the good old age of more than 90 years, still
remembers how full their house was that day, and
how she saw the peach-trees in bloom and the grass
waving, and towards night heard the thunder of the
cannon with which in vain the harassed fugitives
were trying to beat back their pursuers.   Their

* Mrs. Henry Whittemore.
† Mrs. Lydia Peirce.

wives and children provided for — the men of the minute company, I suppose comprising every man in town of suitable age, under command of Captain Benjamin Locke,† met on the common at day-break, and marched to Lexington, ready for any service which might be required. They fought that day, as all the rest, not in military order as a company, but as sharpshooters, each doing the best he could.

At two o'clock in the morning the alarm had been given at Lexington, and the militia and minute men to the number of one hundred and thirty gathered on the common in answer to the summons. The roll was called, the muskets loaded with powder and ball, and as there were no signs of the immediate approach of the British. a watch was set and the company dismissed, to come together at beat of drum. The enemy, seizing every man they met, were undiscovered till they came within a short distance of the village. As their approach became known, the alarm was again sounded. It was now between four and five o'clock. Some sixty or seventy formed on the common in double line, and stood

† See Note A.

there courageously awaiting the result, with orders not to fire unless they were fired upon. They did not wait long; the British advance, having first stopped to load and prime, came in sight hurrying along almost on the run. Pitcairn, a major of the marines, rode in front, and when within five or six rods, cried out, "Disperse, ye villains! Ye rebels, disperse! Lay down your arms, and disperse!"

The main body stood firm, neither laying down their arms nor dispersing. Pitcairn gave the order to fire. At first, came a few scattering shots, and then a deadly volley. Resistance was vain against more than tenfold odds, and Capt. Parker ordered his men to disperse, which they did, firing a few desultory shots, having lost seven killed and ten wounded, a quarter of that gallant band. Thus in the gray of that April morning did American liberty receive its baptism of blood. The die was cast; henceforth colonies no longer. "What a glorious morning is this!" exclaimed Samuel Adams.

The troops formed on the common, fired a volley and gave three cheers in honor of their victory, and, after a halt of half an hour, marched on for Con-

cord, which they entered about 7 o'clock. The
main body remained in the centre of the town, but
about two hundred light infantry were detached to
secure the north bridge on the road leading to
Acton, a hundred of whom went on a mile further
to destroy the stores which were collected at the
house of Col. Barrett. They were not very suc-
cessful in their search, the Americans having
improved the time since the alarm was given in
removing and secreting the military stores. They
destroyed a few barrels of flour, threw five hundred
pounds of ball into a mill pond, knocked off the
trunnions of three iron cannon, burned sixteen
carriage wheels, and a few barrels of wooden
trenchers and spoons. No great return for the
expedition which cost King George the brightest
jewel in his crown, and so many brave men their
lives!

The minute men from the neighboring towns had
been flocking in till more than four hundred were
gathered on the hill above the north bridge. From
this spot they could see the movements of the troops,
and several fires were visible in the village. They

determined to march to the defence of the town.
As they approached the bridge in double file, with
trailed arms, the British began to take up the
planks; and as the Americans quickened their step
to prevent this, first a few scattering shots, and
then a volley, was fired upon them, killing two and
wounding others, — the British, no doubt, expecting
to repeat the easy slaughter of Lexington.   The
volley was returned, and two of the British were
killed and others wounded.   They retreated in
disorder, pursued by the militia over the bridge, —
and this is the famous battle of Concord.

At noon, Col. Smith, observing the rapid increase
of the militia, thought it prudent to commence his
march to Boston.   It was not too soon.   The
minute men were flocking in from the neighboring
towns, and a perilous road was before them through
an aroused and hostile country.   The main column
left Concord a little after twelve o'clock, covered
by a strong flanking guard on the ridge of the hill
to their left.   At Merriam's corner an attack was
made, and a severe skirmish ensued, in which several
of the British were killed.   The Americans, after

this, fought each man for himself; every wall formed a breastwork; every thicket on that hilly, narrow, woody road a fort, till it seemed to the British, as one of their officers wrote, that the walls were " lined with fire," and the hills swarmed with rebels " as if they dropped from the clouds." As they passed along the high ground in Lincoln, the men of Woburn came in, one hundred and eighty strong and the fight raged fiercely. The march began to assume the appearance of a flight. Col. Smith, the commander, was severely wounded while urging on his troops. As they descended the hill into the village of Lexington, the provincials pressed still more closely upon them; and, weary with the long march, encumbered by many wounded, their ammunition almost exhausted, they hurried by the scene of the morning's butchery almost in headlong rout. About two o'clock, a mile below the church, the officers pressed their way to the front, and, by threats of instant death, succeeded in forming the ranks once more, under a deadly fire. The whole force must have surrendered speedily had not relief arrived.

3

Gen. Gage had received early in the morning the request for reinforcements despatched by Col. Smith as he passed through West Cambridge, and at nine o'clock twelve hundred men with two field-pieces, under command of Lord Percy, marched out through Roxbury, in derision of the Americans, to the tune of Yankee Doodle. The men of that time used to say that the British went out playing Yankee Doodle, and came back dancing it.*

The appearance of this strong detachment still further excited the fears of the few who remained in their homes upon our main street. A little girl, named Nabby Blackington, as they marched by, was watching her mother's cow while she fed by the road-side; the cow took her way directly through the passing column, and the child, faithful to her trust, followed through the ranks bristling with bayonets. "We will not hurt the child," they said.† Deacon Ephraim Cutter used to tell his grand-children how, when he was a boy eight years old. he heard the measured tread of the soldiers as of

* Mrs. Lydia Peirce.
† Mrs. Amos Whittemore.

one man, and saw the burnished arms and bright
bayonets glittering in the sunlight, looking like a
flowing river.*

Lord Percy's reinforcement had been delayed for
a little time at Brighton bridge, the planks of
which had been taken up by the direction of the
Committee of Safety. But, unfortunately, they were
simply piled up on the Cambridge side, and it was
the work of but a few moments to replace them
sufficiently to allow the troops to pass. When,
however, a convoy of provisions and supplies in
charge of a sergeant's guard, following in the rear
of the main body, came to the bridge, they could
not cross so easily; and, in the delay incident to
making it passable by the heavy wagons, and misled by false direction as to the road, they became
so far separated from the troops that they could
receive no protection from them. Meantime an
express was sent post-haste from Old Cambridge to
Menotomy, bearing the information that these supplies were on the way. Several of our men met at
once in Cooper's tavern, which stood on the present

* Mrs. Henry Whittemore.

site of Whittemore's hotel, to form some plan for capturing them. They were of the exempts, or alarm list as it was called, all old men, for every young man was that day nearer the post of danger. There were Jason Belknap and Joe Belknap, James Budge, Israel Mead and Ammi Cutter, David Lamson, and others, in all about twelve. Some of them had been soldiers in the French war, and age had not impaired their courage. They chose for their leader David Lamson, a mulatto, who had served in the war, a man of undoubted bravery and determination. They took their position (just here to the right) behind a bank wall of earth and stones, between the present dwellings of Col. Thomas Russell and George C. Russell. The convoy soon made its appearance. As it came between them and the meeting-house of the First Parish, Lamson ordered his men to rise and aim directly at the horses, and called out to them to surrender. No reply was made, but the drivers whipped up their teams. Lamson's men then fired, killing several of the horses, and, according to some accounts, killing

two of the men and wounding others.* One of the
bullets passed through the front door of the church.
The frightened drivers leaped from their places, and,
with the guards, ran directly to the shore of Spy
Pond, into which they threw their guns. One of
them, however, it is said, bent his up over a stone-
wall, as they had been ordered, at all events, not to
allow their arms to be serviceable to the "rebels."
They then followed the westerly shore of the pond,
till, near Spring Valley, they met an old woman,
named mother Batherick, digging dandelions, to
whom they surrendered themselves, asking her protection. She led them to the house of Capt.
Ephraim Frost, where there was a party of our
men, saying to her prisoners, as she gave them up,
"If you ever live to get back, you tell King George
that an old woman took six of his grenadiers prisoners."† They were kindly treated till exchanged.

* A hand-bill with forty coffins at its head, one in memory of
each of the Americans slain, distributed in the country shortly
after the battle, mentions this number, adding that one of the
killed was a lieutenant, who had come out with the convoy for
recreation and to view the country.

† Dr. Benjamin Cutter.

3 *

The squib went the rounds of the English opposition papers, "If one old Yankee woman can take six grenadiers, how many soldiers will it require to conquer America?"

Meanwhile, our people lost no time in securing their prize. The wagons were drawn down into the hollow, just northeast of the Railroad Station, where any one took from them what he wanted. A boy thirteen years old thinking he might take something as well as the rest, secured a soldier's pack and blanket, and with his prize hurried off to his mother, who was at the Whittemore house near Mystic river. When they saw what he had, they would not even allow him to enter the house, they were so fearful that they would thus draw upon themselves the vengeance of the British.

It was probably the officer of this convoy who was seen dead just behind the old Adams house; they knew it was an officer, they said, for his "buttons were all quarters of a dollar."* The marks of blood upon the road were effaced, and the living horses driven over to Medford; and as for the

* Mrs. Lydia Peirce.

dead ones, Rev. Mr. Cooke thought it might expose
the town to the vengeance of the troops on their
return, if these were left in sight, and he with others·
dragged them over to the field just this side of
Spring valley, where the bones lay bleaching for
many years.*   Col. Thomas Russell, to whom I am
indebted for almost the whole of this incident, he
having heard it from the lips of David Lamson and
other actors in the affair, remembers well, when a
lad, playing with those old bones, and throwing
some of them over into the pond.

So to West Cambridge belongs the honor of
making the first capture of provisions and stores,
and also of prisoners, in the American Revolution.

As some of the party were returning home, after
the capture, at Mill street they met Lieut. Edward
Thoroton Gould of the Fourth, or "King's Own,"
Regiment of foot, who having been wounded in the
ankle at Concord bridge, was coming back to Boston alone on horseback.   They took him prisoner,

* Miss Bradshaw, grand-daughter of Mr. Cooke.

and carried him first to Ammi Cutter's, and afterwards to Medford. *

It was about two o'clock in the afternoon when
the reinforcement under Lord Percy met the har-
rassed fugitives from Concord. Percy placed his
field-pieces on the brow of the hill beyond the Mon-
roe tavern, a mile below the Lexington church, and
formed his forces into a hollow square within which
he received the worn-out soldiers. " They lay down
on the ground, with their tongues hanging from their
mouths, like dogs after a chase."

Lord Percy had now under his command about
eighteen hundred veteran troops, the very flower of
the British army, — and yet he did not deem it safe
to tarry long. After a half hour's rest the retreat
was resumed. The light infantry and grenadiers
formed the advance, — the wounded were carried
in the centre in such vehicles as they could seize, —
while the fresh troops furnished the flanking parties
and brought up the rear. From that time their

* Lieut. Gould's affidavit was among the depositions taken
under the direction of the Provincial Congress, and forwarded to
England immediately after the battle, by a swift vessel.

retreat was marked by indiscriminate pillage and wanton destruction. The strong flanking guards on either side gave them opportunity for violence and plunder. Hardly a dwelling on their way escaped. On the summit of what we call "Peirce's Hill" was a house occupied by Mr. Robbins. The family had fled on the approach of the enemy. The flank guard ransacked the premises, destroyed the clock, and set a fire on the kitchen floor, which was extinguished by the wet clothes falling upon it, after it had burned off the lines.*

They broke into what is now the upper end of the old tavern, where Mr. Cutler, a rich farmer and butcher, then lived. The family had all gone to a place of safety, and the soldiers carried off what they could, left the taps of the molasses and spirit casks open, destroyed furniture, drove a bayonet through the best mirror, the frame of which is still preserved,† pillaged the drawers, and set the house on fire. A faithful slave, however, had watched from a safe distance the proceedings, and, as soon as the soldiers left, extinguished the flames.

* Mrs. Lydia Peirce.
† Thomas Hall.

Dea. Joseph Adams, who knew that his life would be in danger, both on account of his name, and also from his reputation for patriotic zeal, but thinking that they would not harm women and children, as the troops came in sight left his house, now occupied by Henry J. Locke, (the original house still standing, as the present L part,) and fled across the fields. He was hotly pursued, and, as he was running under the cover of the stone walls, he heard the bullets whistle over his head. He kept on, however, and had just time to cover himself over in the hay-loft in Rev. Mr. Cooke's barn, (still standing and owned by Miss Bradshaw,) when his pursuers came up and began to search for him, sticking their bayonets here and there into the hay. They did not dare to remain long, and he escaped.*

Meantime a detachment of the soldiers had burst open the doors and entered his house. The five children had hidden under the bed, and on it was lying the mother with her infant, but little more than a fortnight old.† A soldier opened the curtains·

* Miss Bradshaw.
† The infant many of us remember as Mrs. James Hill.

1781168

ADDRESS.

and pointed his bayonet at her breast; she cried out
for mercy, and another soldier who stood near, said,
"We will not hurt the woman if she will go out of
the house, but we will surely burn it." She threw
a blanket over her, and with her infant in her arms,
crawled to the corn-barn close by, while they proceeded with their work of pillage.* They emptied
the drawers into sheets, made bundles of the most
valuable things, and even took out the machinery of
the old clock, the case of which still remains an
heir-loom in the family. The children were not
disturbed in their retreat, and from beneath the bed
watched the feet of the soldiers moving about the
room. Joel Adams, a boy of nine years old, curi-
osity getting the better of his fears, lifted up a
corner of the valance, to get a better view of the
strange proceedings in their home. A soldier saw
him, and said, "Why don't you come out here?"
The boy answered, "You'll kill me if I do." "No
we won't," the soldier replied, and the boy came out
of his hiding-place, and followed them round. His
father was deacon of the church, and had charge of

* See Note B.

the communion service. Joel saw them take his
mother's spoons and other valuables without a word,
but when they proceeded to take possession of the
sacred utensils, he could restrain himself no longer,
and in horror and indignation cried out, " Don't you
touch them 'ere things! Daddy 'l lick you, if you
do." Much to the boy's surprise, the threat was
disregarded; the communion service, and with it the
silver tankard given to the church in 1769 by Jonathan Butterfield, was carried to Boston and pawned
to a silversmith by the name of Austin. Seeing by
the inscription from whence it came, he informed
Dea. Adams where it was, and that he could have it
for the price paid the soldiers. After the evacua-
tion of Boston the two deacons redeemed it at their
own expense, and restored it to the church; and on
every communion day that same silver tankard
stands on the table, as we remember our Master.
After the British had nearly stripped the house they
emptied a basket of chips, which stood by, upon the
middle of the floor, put a brand from the fire-place
into them, broke up and piled on the top the flag-
bottomed chairs, and left the house to destruction.

The fire was extinguished by the children, at the
expense of a pot of home-brewed beer, and with
water from a cask outside, but not until the floor
was badly burned, the ceiling well smoked, and even
the pewter plates melted on the dresser.*

Jason Russell lived in what is now called the
Teel house, the main part of which, with its solid
oak timbers cut between the house and the church,
is very little changed since that time. Being old
and lame he had started at noon with his wife and
children to go up for safety to George Prentiss' on
the hill, but after proceeding a little way he let them
go on alone, and came back to look after things at
home. He barricaded his gate with bundles of
shingles, making what he thought would be a good
cover from which to fire on the enemy as they
returned. Ammi Cutter, his neighbor, came from
his house across the brook to see Mr. Russell, and
advised him to go to a place of greater security.
He refused, saying, "An Englishman's house is his

* Mrs. Thomas Hall, grand-daughter of Mrs. Adams. Rev.
Mr. Brown's sermon on James Hill. S. G. Damon's article in
Christian Register, Oct. 28, 1854.

4

castle." Mr. Cutter left him, and as he was getting over the wall on the other side of the road, he saw the advance of the flanking party close behind him. He ran, and stumbling fell between the logs at the old mill, the bullets striking off the bark upon him. They thought he was dead and passed on. The flanking party south of the road had, meanwhile, made a circuit along the foot of the hill, and driven in the Americans who unsuspiciously were lying in wait there, pressing them down upon the main body. Finding no other chance of escape, they rushed into Mr. Russell's house. Mr. Russell himself, being lame, was the last to reach the house, and was shot with two bullets in his own doorway; they found afterwards eleven bayonet stabs on the body of the poor old man. The soldiers rushed in, killing all they could find concealed in various parts of the house. The Beverly men and some others, eight in all, fled to the cellar, and pointing their guns up the stairs, threatened instant death to any one who should come down, and they escaped. One English-man was shot on the cellar stairs, and another else-where on the premises. After plundering the house they went away leaving our men in the cellar safe,—not venturing down that narrow way, which was certain death to the first who attempted it. Our people gathered up the Americans who were killed in and about the house, and laid them side by side in the south room, and when Mrs. Russell came back to her home she found there, weltering in their own blood, her husband and eleven others. She said the blood in that room was almost ankle deep. The house itself was riddled with bullets, and the marks of them in many places are still visible. The same blood-stained floor remained on that room till a year ago.*

It was probably here that seven of the Danvers men were killed. They had gone into a walled enclosure, and piled bundles of shingles to strengthen their breast-work, and while there were surprised by the flank guard.†

Rev. Mr. Cooke, now nearly seventy years old, was a marked man, because he had been so out-

* Col. Thomas Russell and Mrs. Teel, grandchildren of Jason Russell.

† D. P. King's address at Danvers.

spoken in the cause of freedom. And when one, watching on the hill just behind the parsonage, reported that he saw the bayonets glistening on the Lexington road, his son Samuel took the old gentleman, much against his will, into the chaise, and carried him over to Mr. Clarke's, in the edge of Watertown. Mr. Cooke owned the only white horse, and the only chaise in town,* and the story is told of the little boy, who, when he saw that chaise coming, hid behind the wall in veneration and awe of the minister. The parsonage, owned now by Miss Bradshaw, a grand-daughter of Mr. Cooke, was used as a hospital after the battle, and the stain of blood is still on the floor, where they lifted in a wounded man at the window.† There is also the hole of a bullet through the shutter, and, in fact, nearly all the houses then standing on the street were thus marked.

As the troops continued their retreat, they plundered the house next above the Universalist church, trampled to pieces on the floor the year's stock of

* Mrs. Lydia Peirce.
† Miss Bradshaw.

candles which had just been made, smashed in the
panels of a book-case which is still in existence,
and left the building on fire. They entered the
little store then kept on the corner of Water Street
by Thomas Russell (the great-grandfather of Thomas
Henry Russell, who now has his store on the same
spot), carrying away and destroying what they
could, and leaving the taps of the barrels of
molasses and liquor open. The old Adams house,
which a few years ago stood close to the station,
received its full share of honorable bullet-marks,
being first in full range of the American, and then
of the British, fire. It is said that one man, surprised in this house, saved his life by climbing up
into the big chimney, and standing on the cross-pole
from which the kettles were hung. It was about
four o'clock in the afternoon when the main body
passed through the centre of West Cambridge, and
here the fight grew more desperate. The Americans began to lose their fear of the cannon, and,
after they descended from the high ground near the
"Foot of the Rocks," had pressed closer upon the
shattered ranks of the enemy. The militia from

4 *

the lower towns came in. Gen. Heath, who took
command of our people at Lexington, tried to bring
into military order the scattered provincials, and
Joseph Warren was everywhere in the thickest of
the fight, urging them on; indeed, he narrowly
escaped with his life, a bullet passing so near his
head that it struck the " pin out of the hair of his
ear-lock." *

Here Samuel Whittemore was left for dead. He
was awakened in the night in his house under the
great elms, and, as we mentioned before, looking
out saw the bayonets glistening in the moonlight.
His wife, early in the morning, made her preparations to go for safety to her son's house near
Mystic River, and, when she was ready, she looked
around for her husband, thinking that, of course, as
he was more than eighty years old he would go
with her. She found him oiling his musket and
pistols, and sharpening his sword, for in his
younger days he had been an officer in the militia.
She urged him to go with her; but no, he was
"going up in town." As the British on their

* Memoirs of Gen. Heath.

retreat were passing through the centre, they
halted a moment by the church. He lay under
cover of a wall near where the Russell school-house
now stands, and fired some half dozen shots at the
enemy. He had just loaded his gun, when he
heard the wall rattle and saw five soldiers of the
flank-guard approaching him shoulder to shoulder.
Beside being eighty years old he was lame, and
knew that it was of no use to attempt to escape.
With his musket he shot one of the soldiers, and,
instantly drawing his pistol, fired at another. He
aimed the second pistol and discharged it just as
they fired at him; one of the soldiers was seen to
clap his hand to his breast. As he fired the third
time a ball struck him in the head, and he fell sense-
less. The soldiers beat him with their muskets,
bayoneted him, and left him for dead. After the
British had passed by, our people, finding that
there was some life left in him, carried him to
Cooper's tavern, where the surgeon, Dr. Tufts of
Medford, said that it was useless to dress his
wounds, for he could not live. He dressed the
wounds however, and the old hero lived eighteen

years after this, dying in 1793 at the age of 98. The people of that time accounted for his longevity by saying that "He bled like an ox" from his wounds, and through the new blood formed got a new lease of life. A woman in Boston, who was acquainted with people here, heard the soldiers, next day, saying "We killed an old devil there in Menotomy, but we paid most too dear for it, — lost three of our men, the last died this morning." The old lady, when her husband was recovering, could not forbear saying (as even the best wives sometimes will say), "Well, now, don't you wish you had done as I wanted you to do?" "No," said he, "I would run the same chance again." *

Seth Russell and Samuel Frost, of West Cambridge, were taken prisoners. They put Frost on a horse, and cut his waist-band strings so that he could not easily run away. They were carried on board a guard-ship in the harbor, and were soon afterwards exchanged.

Jabez Wyman and Jason Winship, though entirely unarmed, were most barbarously killed and muti-

* F. H. Whittemore.

lated in Cooper's tavern. They had come up to inquire the news, and were surprised there. The landlady, Mrs. Cooper, who was just mixing flip at the bar, with her husband fled to the cellar.† A part of the old tavern-building was moved next to Mr. Fowle's house, and stood there till within a few years; the marks of the bullets were still to be seen on its walls.

Edward Hall, 1st Lieut. of the Royal 43d Regiment, was wounded in the arm at Concord, and was brought down in a chaise in the centre of the troops. The horse was not so swift as the men, and falling a little into the rear he was wounded again, in the shoulder, this time mortally, near Samuel Butterfield's. When Mrs. Butterfield, who lived on the north side of the road, returned to her own house she found her best bed covered with blood and occupied by this British officer, and a wounded Provincial (Hemmenway of Framingham,) in the other bed. The American recovered, but the officer lingered along a fortnight and then died having received every attention from his hostess; supplies,

† See note C.

also, and nurses for him, were sent out from Boston
with a flag of truce. One of our people came into
the house, and upbraiding Mrs. Butterfield as a tory,
because she harbored her country's enemy, threatened to kill him. She told the man, "Only cowards
would want to kill a dying man."*

Through their whole retreat the British had
noticed one man in particular, whom they learned
especially to dread. He was an old, gray-haired
hunter, named Wyman of Woburn, and he rode a
fine white horse. He struck the trail as they left
Concord, and would ride up within gunshot, then
turning the horse throw himself off, aim his long
gun resting on the saddle, and that aim was death.
They would say, " Look out, there is the man on the
white horse." He followed them the whole distance,
and James Russell, the father of James Russell, Esq.,
then a boy of a dozen years, from behind a house
on Charlestown street, saw him gallop across the
brook and up the hill, pursued by a party of the
flank guard who kept the plains midway between
Charlestown and Main streets. He turned, aimed,

---

* Miss Deborah Butterfield, daughter of Mrs. B.

and the boy saw one of the British fall. He rode on, and soon the same gun was heard again, this time also with deadly effect.*

Lieut. Bowman met at North Cambridge a soldier who had straggled some distance away from his comrades. It was man to man in single combat, and it happened that neither gun was loaded. The Briton rushed at his antagonist with fixed bayonet; nothing daunted Bowman awaited the attack with clubbed musket, and striking aside the bayonet with one blow felled the soldier to the ground and took him prisoner.†

The Whittemore boys, Jonathan and Josiah, were sitting on a fence at some distance from the road, watching what they thought was the pretty sight of gaily dressed soldiers passing by, till a bullet struck the rail just below them, and Josiah dropped off, exclaiming in his fright, "I'm dead," which was a byword in the family for many years. The children ran away at the top of their speed to the swamps behind the house, where they spent the whole night.‡

* Thomas Hall. James Russell, Esq.
† Dr. B. Cutter.
‡ F. H. Whittemore.

And thus the British passed again beneath those old elm trees, not proudly as in the morning, but fugitives from those they had despised, war-worn and weary, harassed on every side, their officers on foot to escape the deadly aim of the American marksmen, their centre encumbered with wagons bearing their wounded, and they had left many brave comrades on the hills of Lexington and on the plains of West Cambridge slain in behalf of an unjust cause. More were killed on both sides within our limits than in any other town: at least twenty-two of the Americans, and probably more than twice that number of the British, fell in West Cambridge. They hurried along, and only their speed and the delay of Col. Pickering, who was coming up with the fine Essex regiment of seven hundred men, saved them from total rout. As it was, the remnant of the proud army reached Charlestown Neck, and sought shelter under the guns of the ships of war about sunset, having lost in killed, wounded and missing, two hundred and seventy-three men. The. Americans lost that day forty-nine killed, thirty-four wounded and five missing.

Before the next evening the British were besieged
in Boston by an army probably numbering ten thousand men. The whole country was represented in
this besieging force. The men all started from my
native town in New Hampshire, on foot or on horseback as they were able, as soon as the report came
to them that the regulars were on the road. Though
the town of Peterboro' contained then but seventy
or eighty families, twenty-two of her citizens were
present at the battle of Bunker Hill,—and when
the news of that battle reached the town every able-
bodied man with such weapons as he could procure
was on the march. Those on foot marched twenty
miles and then hearing the result turned back, but
those on horseback proceeded as far as West Cambridge, where they passed the night in a large
vacant house.

As we sum up the anguish and distresses of that
day, we must not think that those who actively
engaged in the conflict were the only sufferers. It
may be that the wives and mothers of our town
suffered yet more. From their places of safety on
the hills they could hear the din of the battle, and

5

they knew not but each sharp volley, each cannon
shot, carried death to him they loved. All sorts of
exaggerated and unfounded reports reached them
of the doings of the day. Vague rumors were
afloat of plots and conspiracies. The report was
spread abroad that the slaves were intending to
rise, and finish what the British had begun by
murdering the defenceless women and children.
It excited great consternation, therefore, among
the women gathered at George Prentiss's upon the
hill, when they saw Ishmael, a negro slave belonging
to Mr. Cutler, approaching the house. They thought
their time had come, but one, a little braver than
the rest, summoned up courage to ask, " Are you
going to kill us, Ishmael ? " " Lord-a-massy, no
ma'am ! " said the astonished black. " Is my missis
here ? " *

There was room for a little mingling of ro-
mance even in such scenes. John Tufts had come
up from his home in Somerville to take his part
in the events of the day. He chanced to meet a
young woman, Elizabeth Perry by name, wandering

* Mrs. Lydia Peirce.

in the fields in a state of great anxiety and fear. The young man, though he had never seen her before, gallantly offered his protection, which she thankfully accepted; and, as for the result, it need only be said that her name afterwards became Elizabeth Tufts.*

There was sadness and sorrow in these homes when the people returned to them, after the enemy had passed by. Strange scenes met their eyes. As Mrs. Adams came back to what we used to call the "Old Adams House," she was obliged to step over the dead body of a British soldier, in order to enter her back door. And in the front room lay another soldier mortally wounded, the white sanded floor beneath him red with the blood which had flowed through the bed from his wounds. She at once set to work to make him more comfortable, preparing food which might serve to revive him; but he lived only a few hours. Our wounded were carried to the tavern, to the church, to the parsonage, to the houses near where they fell.

In the consternation and fear of that hour, the

* Oliver Tufts.

dead were placed on a sled, and drawn by a yoke of oxen upon the bare ground to the grave-yard. A single grave was hastily dug, and the twelve were laid in it side by side, "head to point," with their clothes on just as they fell.* A few years ago, when they opened the mound, to lay the foundation of a monument in honor of the patriot dead, they found there, mingled with that sacred dust, the remains of the socks and garments, which, through the long nights of that anxious winter, wives and mothers had been making for those they loved. Little thought those wives and mothers that their work would be treasured as a precious relic; little thought those brave men, amid the smoke and toil and agony of that day, that they would be revered as heroes and martyrs by a great nation. As with tender reverence we look back to the days of 1775, so will those who come after us look back to these crowded months which we are living now. Let us see to it, my friends, that we do no act and speak no word which shall give our children and our children's children cause for bitter shame!

* Col. Thomas Russell.

A simple slate-stone marked the spot where they rested, and it stands there still, by the side of the monument which was erected by our citizens in 1848.

The British dead were, many of them, buried near the wall and close to the brook which runs through the old grave-yard, in the spot used for the burial-place of the slaves. Tradition says that the grave of one British soldier is in the valley between my house and Pleasant Street. Rev. Mr. Cooke, in his record of the year, sums up thus his account of deaths: "1775, died and buried in this precinct, ah! forty-seven, besides some Provincials and Hutchinson's butchers, slain in Concord battle, near this meeting-house; buried here."

Many tears were shed on the next Sabbath, as the little flock met for worship in the village church. There were the vacant seats which the dead had filled. There were the widows and orphans who the Sabbath before had met in joy. And, most touching sight, there was Anna, the infant grand-daughter of Jason Russell, born on the very day of the battle; and the infant son of Jason Winship, brought to

5 *

the altar for baptism, while the grandfather and the father were lying in their bloody shrouds in the church-yard close by.

On a sermon of Rev. Mr. Cooke, in my possession, I find this brief note. "This prepared for April 23d, 1775. Lexington battle and plunder prevented." Probably, that day, he uttered the thoughts which gushed fresh out of his heart. No wonder that the spirit of the good pastor was stirred within him, and he wrote in his journal the fervent prayer, "Scatter, O Lord, those who delight in blood! For the sighing of the oppressed and needy, make bare thine almighty arm for their help! Teach our hands to war, ah, and our fingers to fight, since in thy providence we are called to this!"

I have thus attempted to relate to you the incidents of that eventful day, which gave to us a country. And they come to us with peculiar appropriateness now, while in the agony of a terrible war we are striving to keep what they then began to win. Our town at that time earned an honorable fame; let us see to it that we do not disgrace it!

I hope the name of the town will never be

changed. It would be like giving up our birthright. As the Second Precinct of Cambridge, we hold an honorable place in history; who would alienate that inheritance? Other names may be more euphonious, but as soon should the man give up his surname, consecrated by the good acts, and glorified by the patriotism of pious and brave ancestors, as we give up that good old name of Cambridge, with which our village was baptized in blood on the nineteenth of April.

We, my friends, must take that name, already honored, and make it yet more bright and honorable, by brave deeds in the field and Christian help in the hospital. Let our soldiers take it with them in this second war for Independence, as a trust not yet tarnished by cowardice, illustrated so recently by heroic death. Let our ladies inscribe that name upon what they send, so that the blessing of the wounded and the prayer of the dying may lisp it gratefully.

NOTES

NOTE A—PAGE 16.

We cannot ascertain with exactness the population of this precint at the time. In 1781 an assessment was made for the supply of beef to the army, and there were one hundred and thirty-three who paid the poll-tax.[*]

Among the papers of Capt. Benjamin Locke [†] are the original enlistment-rolls of the company, with the signatures, and also a list of the members with their places of residence in Capt. Locke's handwriting. The following is a copy of the articles of enlistment:

"We, the subscribers, do hereby solemnly and severally engage and inlist ourselves as soldiers in the Massachusetts Service, for the Preservation of the Liberties of America, from the Day of our Inlistment to the last Day of December next, unless the Service should admit of a Discharge of a Part or the Whole sooner, which shall be at the Discretion of the Committee of Safety, and we

---

[*] Dr. B. Cutter.

[†] Now in the possession of the widow of his grandson, the late Delmont Locke.

. hereby promise to submit ourselves to all the Orders and
Regulations of the Army, and faithfully to observe and
obey all such Orders as we shall receive from Time to
Time, from our superior Officers."

The names on the various rolls are thus brought
together by Capt. Locke in his list of the members:

" Seth Stone, Cambridge.
 Thos. Cutter, Jr., Cambridge.
 James Fowle, Cambridge.
 Jonathan Perry, Cambridge.
 Joseph Frost, Cambridge.
 Daniel Cutter, Charlestown.
 Abraham Hill, Cambridge.
 Job Potamea, Stoneham.
 Josiah Williams, Cambridge.
 Miles Greenwood, Cambridge.
 Matthew Cox, Cambridge.
 Moses Hovey, Cambridge.
 Peter Stearns, Cambridge.
 Ephraim Mullet, Charlestown.
 John Fowle, Cambridge.
 John Shelden Senter, Charlestown
 John Lock, Cambridge.

Israel Blackinton, Jr., Cambridge.

William Dickson, Charlestown.

Andrew Cutter, Cambridge.

Elisha Hastings, Cambridge.

Joseph Cox, Cambridge.

Isaac Fillebrown. Charlestown.

Joseph Trask, Boston.

William Pradex, Boston.

John Stewart.

Samuel Pierce, Jr., Boston.

John Grimes, Boston.

William Hopkins, Charlestown.

Richard Loring, Charlestown.

Ebenezer Cox, Boston.

John Cutter, Cambridge.

William Adams, Cambridge.

Zachariah Hill, Cambridge.

Samuel Peirce, Charlestown.

John Tidd, Cambridge.

Andrew Mallet, Charlestown.

Israel Blackinton, Cambridge.

William Winship, Cambridge.

David Blodget, Stoneham.

Joseph Robinson. Lexington.

Charles Cutter, Cambridge.

Samuel Seger, Newtown.

Isaiah Berjanah, Stoneham.

Ebenezer Bowman, Lexington.

Richard Ketel, Boston.

* Cuff Whittemore, Cambridge.

William Ellery, Charlestown.

* Cato Wood, Charlestown.

Jonathan Clarke, Boston.

This Company joined in the siege of Boston which immediately followed, and probably was also in the battle of Bunker Hill. Capt. Locke was in that battle, and his musket becoming too hot to hold, by reason of frequent firing, he wound his handkerchief around it, and kept on. After that, they were encamped on Prospect Hill. The following bill is preserved, — for services in returning deserters : —

" *Capt. Locke to Samuel Allen, Dr.*

To cash paid for two of your deserted soldiers, viz., —— —— and —— —— † which I took up in Attle-

---

* Cuff Whittemore and Cato Wood were negroes. It is worthy of notice that the blacks fought, not in separate companies, but side by side with the whites through the Revolutionary War.

† Neither of these men were from West Cambridge.

borough the 24th of July, inst., and brought back to the
camp, 45 miles;

To cash paid which they owed Levi Maxey,	£0	6	10
To do. paid for them at Manns, supper and lodging, drink, &c.	0	4	2
To breakfast, &c., at Chines Tavern,	0	2	2
To paid for them for drink, &c.	0	1	2
To paid 2 men for aid, 45 miles,	0	18	0
To paid ditto their expence,	0	13	6
To 2 horses and one carage,	1	10	0
To my time, expence, and horse keeping,	1	6	0
	£5	1	10

Prospect Hill, July 27th, 1775."

On the back of the bill is the following endorsement:

" CHARLESTOWN, PROSPECT HILL, July 27th, 1775

SIR. I have received the two within-named deserters
at the hands of Mr. Samuel Allen, and if you are the
proper person to pay him, you will please to answer the
within accompt, or direct him where he may receive his
pay.

from your Humble Servt."

They had not left Prospect Hill at the last of the year. for we find these receipts:

"PROSPECK HILL, De ye 26, 1775.

Recevd of Capt. Benjamin Lock By hand of Lieut. Solomon Bowman one pare of shoes, to it six shillings.

JOHN TIDD."

"PROSPICK HILL, De ye 27, 1775.

Recevd of Capt. Benjamin Lock by the hand of Lieut. Solomon Bowman one pare shoes and two pare of stockkins, to it twelve shillings and eight pence.

WILLIAM PRADEX."

—

NOTE B—PAGE 27.

The following deposition was taken by order of the Provincial Congress:

"Hannah Adams, wife of Deacon Joseph Adams, of the second precinct in Cambridge, testifieth and saith that on the nineteenth day of April last, upon the return of the King's troops from Concord, divers of them entered our house by bursting open the doors, and three of the soldiers broke into the room in which I then was. laid on my bed, being scarcely able to walk from my bed to the fire, not having been to my chamber door from my being delivered in child-birth to that time. One of said soldiers immediately opened my curtains with his bayonet fixed pointing the same at my breast. I immediately cried out, " For the Lord's sake, do not kill me!" He replied, " Damn you!" One that stood near said, " We will not hurt the woman, if she will go out of the house, but we will surely burn it." I immediately arose, threw a blanket over me, and crawled into a corn-house near the door with my infant in my arms, where I remained until they were gone. They immediately set the house on fire, in which I had left five children and no other person. but the fire was happily extinguished when the house was in the utmost danger of being utterly consumed.

Cambridge, Second Precinct, 17th May, 1775."

NOTE C—PAGE 31.

" CAMBRIDGE, May 19, 1775.

We, Benjamin Cooper and Rachel Cooper, both of Cambridge, aforesaid, of lawful age, testify and say that in the afternoon of the 19th day of April last, the

6 *

King's regular troops, under the command of General
Gage, upon their return from blood and slaughter, which
they had made at Lexington and Concord, fired more
than a hundred bullets into the house where we dwell,
through doors, windows, &c.; then a number of them
entered the house, where we and two aged gentlemen
were all unarmed. We escaped for our lives into the
cellar; the two aged gentlemen were immediately most
barbarously and inhumanly murdered by them, being
stabbed through in many places, their heads mauled,
skulls broke, and their brains out on the floor and walls
of the house; and further saith not."

www.ingramcontent.com/pod-product-compliance
Lightning Source LLC
Chambersburg PA
CBHW021525090426
42739CB00007B/790